Politics, Publishing and Personalities

Politics, Publishing and Personalities:
Wrexham Newspapers 1848–1914

By Lisa Peters

University of Chester Press

First published 2011
by University of Chester Press
University of Chester
Parkgate Road
Chester CH1 4BJ

Printed and bound in the UK by the
LIS Print Unit
University of Chester
Cover designed by the
LIS Graphics Team
University of Chester

© Lisa Peters, 2011

All Rights Reserved
No part of this publication may be reproduced, stored in a retrieval system or transmitted in any form or by any means without the prior permission of the copyright owner, other than as permitted by current UK copyright legislation or under the terms and conditions of a recognised copyright licensing scheme

A catalogue record for this book is available from the British Library

ISBN 978-1-905929-87-0

CONTENTS

List of Illustrations	vi
Acknowledgements	vii
Introduction	1
Chapter 1 – The Wrexham Area	3
Chapter 2 – Brief History of Provincial Newspapers	8
Chapter 3 – Wrexham's Newspapers	19
Chapter 4 – Inter-Newspaper Rivalry	51
Conclusion	59
Epilogue	60
Appendix	64
Selected Bibliography	66

LIST OF ILLUSTRATIONS

Figure 1:	Wrexham and the pre-1974 counties of North Wales	4
Figure 2:	The main railway lines in the Wrexham area by 1900	7
Figure 3:	Advertising in the *Wrexhamite*	13
Figure 4:	Richard Hughes	19
Figure 5:	*Wrexham Recorder* masthead	21
Figure 6:	George Bayley	22
Figure 7:	*Wrexham Registrar* masthead	22
Figure 8:	Charles George Bayley	23
Figure 9:	Dissenters' Burial Ground in Rhosddu	24
Figure 10:	George Bradley	28
Figure 11:	Bradley Road sign	28
Figure 12:	John Rice Jones	29
Figure 13:	James Lindop	31
Figure 14:	Extract from *The Wrexham Albion*	32
Figure 15:	Local food advertisements in the *Wrexhamite*	34
Figure 16:	Former *Wrexham Telegraph* offices at 18 High Street, Wrexham	36
Figure 17:	*North Wales Guardian* printing works	37
Figure 18:	Sir Watkin Williams Wynn	38
Figure 19:	John Ramsden	39
Figure 20:	Advertisement for *North Wales Guardian* printing services	40
Figure 21:	Sir Evan Morris	41
Figure 22:	Griffith Parry Edwards	42
Figure 23:	Sydney Gardnor Jarman	42
Figure 24:	Peter Walker's obelisk	47
Figure 25:	*Wrexham Argus* masthead	50
Figure 26:	Advertising the *Daily Post* local editions	62

ACKNOWLEDGEMENTS

Photographs of George Bayley, James Lindop, John Rice Jones and George Bradley reproduced with the kind permission of Wrexham Archives Service.

Front cover of the *Wrexham Albion* reproduced with the kind permission of Denbighshire Record Office.

INTRODUCTION

This book is a shortened version of my PhD thesis from the University of Wales, Aberystwyth on Wrexham newspapers in the period between 1848 and 1914. It aims to be a brief introduction to the town's newspapers and the people involved in the production of the publications, with further detailed information available in the thesis.

Since the first provincial newspaper appeared in the early eighteenth century, towns throughout the length and breadth of Britain have enjoyed their own newspapers – some of which have lasted centuries while others, many others, failed to reach their first anniversary. The local press is a microcosm of local society with content ranging from politics and trade to fashions, gossip and weddings, and can reveal much about the town they serve. Wrexham's first newspaper appeared in 1848 and throughout much of the Victorian era the town had two, sometimes three, rival newspapers. Rivalry between a town's newspapers usually added an exciting frisson to the trade – this was certainly true in Wrexham and its Liberal- and Conservative-supporting newspapers traded jibes as they fought for the widest, largest, and most influential circulation. Rivalry was not just limited to Wrexham, as each title's expansion plans brought it into conflict with newspapers in Cheshire, Shropshire, and elsewhere in North Wales.

This is the story of Wrexham's newspapers from their founding until the First World War – their place within a British and Welsh context, the early struggle to develop a weekly newspaper, the growth of some newspapers and the failure of others, the people involved, the role of local politicians, and the rivalries and the squabbles as each title strove to be acknowledged as having the widest, largest, and most influential circulation of any newspaper published in Wrexham. This history, together with its wide range of illustrations, gives a unique perspective on the influential newspaper personalities of the time and shows their lasting significance for the town of Wrexham and its surrounding area.

CHAPTER 1 – THE WREXHAM AREA

Situated some nine miles from the English border, Wrexham was the largest town in North Wales by the late nineteenth century, yet it was overshadowed by the nearby English cities of Chester and Liverpool. In 1841 its population of 5,831 was lower than that of both Bangor and Caernarvon but it grew steadily to reach 10,978 in 1881 and 18,377 in 1911, twice that of Caernarvon, thus making it the largest town in North Wales. Wrexham had been an established market and assize town since the Middle Ages and by 1800 had established itself as the main town of North East Wales. Despite this, Wrexham's administrative importance was not recognised until September 1857 when the town gained its Charter of Incorporation and with it control over its own municipal affairs. It was surrounded by mining villages such as Minera and Rhosllanerchrugog whose livelihood was based on the North Wales coalfield, and Bersham, home of 'Iron Mad' John Wilkinson. Yet Wrexham's influence over North Wales was weak, primarily due to the overshadowing influence of Chester and Liverpool and to a lesser extent, Oswestry, which may have acted to limit the expansion of Wrexham's influence south into Montgomeryshire.

In the Victorian era, much of the area surrounding Wrexham was involved in the coal, iron, and lead industries and the town thus acted as an important commercial and transport centre for nearby areas. Within the town itself, leather and brewing were important industries. The leather industry began to increase in size from the late eighteenth century and production was concentrated upon special grades of leather needed for the rollers of spinning machinery. At the same time the brewing industry increased

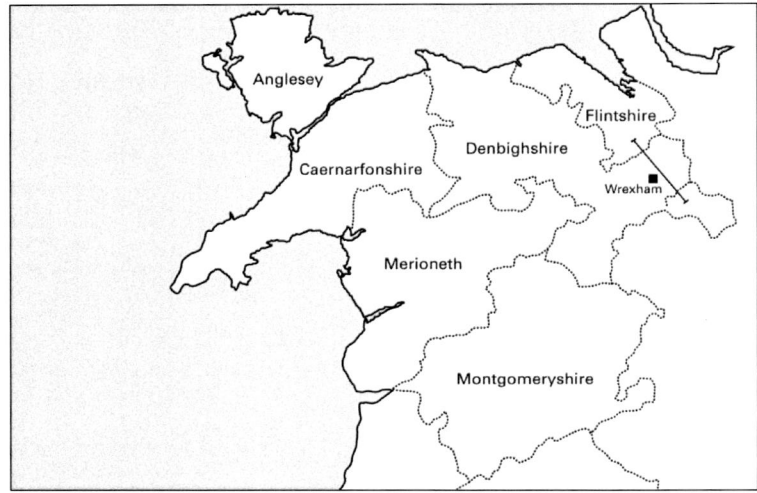

Figure 1: Wrexham and the pre-1974 counties of North Wales.

in size, and by 1850 there were ten to twelve large breweries in the town, serving nearly sixty public houses.

Wrexham had long been recognised as a town where the English language was dominant. Its close proximity to the English border sometimes made it seem more like an English town than a Welsh one. Although anglicised, Wrexham was an important commercial, economic, and industrial centre for both English- and Welsh-speaking North East Wales and became a centre for Welsh Methodism and Welsh cultural movements. Despite these factors, Wrexham remained a predominantly English-speaking town as by 1891 over half of the town's population were monoglot English speakers compared to only one in five monoglot Welsh speakers.

The arrival of the railway brought about a transport revolution in North Wales in the second half of the nineteenth century. Before the railway, coach was the main method of transportation. In the eighteenth century, the roads in North Wales were generally very poor and often impassable during harsh weather, but from the 1750s the situation around Wrexham began to improve. Turnpike trusts, believed to be the first in Wales, were established for the Shrewsbury-Wrexham road in 1752, an example followed throughout Denbighshire and Flintshire so that by 1840 the two counties had eighteen turnpike trusts covering nearly 300 miles of road. In the 1820s coaches left Wrexham daily for Chester, Hereford, Oswestry, Welshpool and Shrewsbury and by 1840 three coaches were leaving for Liverpool each day. Additionally, Wrexham offered daily carrier services to Chester, weekly services to Liverpool, Ellesmere, Llangollen, Bala, Dolgellau, and Llanrwst and thrice weekly services to Mold and Oswestry. Even before the coming of the railway, Wrexham was an important communications centre and possessed relatively well developed road links.

Before the creation of Wrexham's first newspaper in 1848 there were already rail lines between Rhosrobin, Minera, and Brymbo (North Wales Mineral Railway) serving the local mines and quarries, and the Shrewsbury–Chester line which ran through Ruabon and Wrexham. In the same year that the *Wrexham Recorder* and the *Wrexham Registrar* were first published, the Chester–Holyhead railway, running along the North Wales coast, was opened. This line connected the towns of Bangor, Flint, Holywell, and Rhyl, amongst others, to the important city of Chester and consequently to the rest of the British rail network.

After 1848 the number of railway schemes rose dramatically, so that by the early 1870s most of the towns and many of the larger villages of North East Wales and the border area were located on a railway line. The 1850s saw the opening of railway routes connecting Bangor and Caernarvon (1852), and Rhyl and Denbigh (1858), but it was during the 1860s that railways began to proliferate. In 1861 the Vale of Llangollen Railway opened and reached Corwen in 1865. The Denbigh–Ruthin–Corwen Railway, authorised in 1860, reached Ruthin in 1862 and Corwen two years later, and was linked with the Vale of Clwyd line to the coast in 1868 and the Mold–Denbigh line a year later. In 1862 the Wrexham–Minera Railway opened and four years later was extended north to the mines in the Flintshire village of Coed Talon. Possibly the most important railway development of the decade was the opening of the Wrexham, Mold & Connah's Quay Railway in January 1866. This provided a link from Wrexham to the port of Connah's Quay in Flintshire via the industrial villages of Gwersyllt, Caergwrle, Hope, Cefnybedd, and Buckley. This line connected Wrexham, albeit in a roundabout fashion, with west Denbighshire, and the towns of Denbigh, Ruthin, Mold, St Asaph, and Rhuddlan. Wrexham had been connected by rail with Chester and Shrewsbury since the 1840s, and from Chester connections could be made to Birmingham and other English cities as well as to Holyhead and the growing North Wales coastal resorts.

    The arrival of the railway had a major social and economic impact on North Wales and its newspapers. The railways brought news from London and abroad far more quickly than the stagecoach and also allowed newspapers to send copies to settlements further away than previously which, in turn, increased their geographical area of circulation. The railways also brought a threat to the local press in the form of daily London newspapers which now began to appear in the provinces on publication day. Local weekly newspapers were generally unaffected by this, the main threat being to the provincial morning dailies, but it did cause them to become significantly more local in their content as there was no longer any need to report national and international news unless there was a local angle.

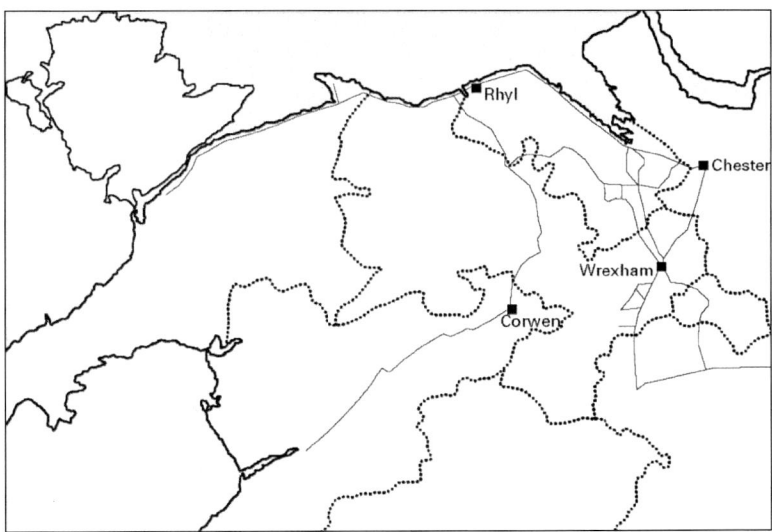

Figure 2: The main railway lines in the Wrexham area by 1900 (in relation to the county boundaries).

CHAPTER 2 – BRIEF HISTORY OF PROVINCIAL NEWSPAPERS

In the UK
In 1695 the lapse of the 1662 Licensing Act, which had restricted printing to London, Oxford, Cambridge and York, paved the way for the creation of newspapers outside these four cities. Printers began to move to provincial towns and cities and at least three provincial newspapers had been established by 1704. Difficulties relating to the survival of these early newspapers make it difficult to state with certainty the identity of the first provincial newspaper but it was probably the *Norwich Post* in 1701, followed by the *Bristol Post Boy* in 1701 or 1702, and *Sam. Farley's Exeter Post-Man* in 1704. These newspapers were all located in older established cities some distance from London but as the century progressed, industrial cities such as Newcastle and Manchester expanded in size and began to establish their own newspapers.

Concerned by the potential power of newspapers, the government took action to limit the influence of the press, especially the hostile press, and confine circulation to the upper and middle classes, by introducing the 'taxes on knowledge': stamp duty, advertising duty, and paper duty. In 1712 Parliament passed the Stamp Act which placed a tax on newspapers known as stamp duty. The charge was a penny per sheet but the Act was poorly drafted and offered newspapers a loophole, namely, that no rate was stated for newspapers printed on one and a half sheets. Newspapers adopted this format and successfully argued that they were pamphlets and were therefore taxed at three shillings per edition as opposed to one and a half pence per issue. This loophole led to a growth in provincial newspapers until it was closed by the 1725 Stamp Act.

Table 1: Stamp Duty, 1712–1855.

Date	Stamp Duty (per sheet)
1712	1*d*.
1776	1 ½*d*.
1789	2*d*.
1797	3 ½*d*.
1815	4*d*.
1836	1*d*.
1855	abolished

Stamp duty peaked at four pence at the end of the Napoleonic Wars, having risen over the past century. As a result of the proliferation of unstamped newspapers in the 1830s, duty fell by three-quarters in 1836 to one penny and this concession spurred on the campaign to abolish the duty which was led by the Newspaper Stamp Abolition Committee, established in 1849. Stamp duty was especially harsh on provincial newspapers as the stamped paper had to come from London and, to avoid running out of paper, provincial newspapers in distant areas or with poor communication links were obliged to keep an excessively large supply in stock and this took up storage space and caused financial problems.

A second 'tax on knowledge' was advertising duty which commenced at the same time as stamp duty. Advertising was an important source of revenue for newspapers and remains an important source today. It was finally abolished in 1853, after peaking at three shillings and six pence per advertisement in 1815. The abolition of paper duty in 1861 marked the end of the 'taxes on knowledge'.

Table 2: Advertising Duty, 1712–1853.

Date	Advertisement Duty (per advertisement)
1712	1s.
1757	2s.
1780	2s. 6d.
1789	3s.
1815	3s. 6d.
1833	1s. 6d.
1853	abolished

Despite these taxes, the number of provincial newspapers slowly increased. Numbers rose from around twenty-five in 1735 to thirty-five by 1760 and over fifty by the early 1780s. By 1830 there were over 150 provincial newspapers in England alone. However the provincial press displayed a high casualty rate – the 'taxes on knowledge' meant that newspapers were usually only marginally profitable – and most nineteenth-century provincial newspaper proprietors were printers whose first concern was their printing business. Some 130 newspapers were launched outside London between 1701 and 1760, but only around half of these existed for at least five years. In addition, some large cities had several newspapers while others had none at all.

Surprisingly, many early provincial newspapers carried very little local news, primarily because proprietors were concerned with offending local dignitaries. Consequently court reports, which were a popular part of the limited local news coverage, tended to concentrate on the crimes of the working class. During wartime, foreign news was naturally of great interest, especially if the UK was involved in the conflict and manuscript letters from local residents detailing foreign news were especially interesting to readers. Editorial work generally consisted of cutting and pasting articles from London or other provincial newspapers. Feature articles, including poems and stories, were a popular component of these weeklies and often offered a local aspect as many of the contributors were readers of the newspaper.

The repeal of the various 'taxes on knowledge' from 1853 onwards significantly altered the provincial press. Newspapers could now offer their lowest price to readers, usually the 'popular penny' and this led to a dramatic expansion in readership and the number of newspapers. The years after 1855 saw the rise of the provincial morning daily newspaper with major cities including Manchester, Birmingham, Leeds and Edinburgh, having a least two by the 1880s. However, from the 1880s the provincial morning dailies were eclipsed by the rise of their evening counterparts. Evening newspapers tended to be a compilation of telegraph news, in particular sporting information. As the provincial halfpenny evening market expanded, the number of penny morning newspapers fell. Attempts were made to revitalise the morning market by the introduction of halfpenny morning dailies, starting with the *Northern Echo* in 1870, but by 1910 morning dailies were outnumbered by the evening press. Nevertheless, the English press remained numerically dominated by the weekly, as only large settlements could support a daily newspaper. Weeklies also remained the dominant newspaper type in Wales whose daily press was restricted to the south.

There were several reasons for the continued success of provincial newspapers, both daily and weekly, after 1855.

Firstly, in addition to national and foreign news coverage, they provided local and regional news. Secondly, they were able, crucially, to attract local, regional, and national advertising. After 1853 advertising became an increasingly important source of revenue for provincial newspapers, especially the smaller weeklies. Despite the power of advertising, newspapers initially accepted it reluctantly and were loath to admit that advertisements (or the lack of them) usually determined a newspaper's success or failure. Consequently, advertisements were not allowed to break columns or to include illustrations or different types of lettering until the 'New Journalism' of the 1880s. Thirdly, in the second half of the nineteenth century several technical advances in printing greatly aided newspaper production. The larger and more prosperous newspapers, starting with *The Times* in 1866, moved from Hoe four- or six-feeders to web-fed rotaries. Wood pulp (newsprint) began to be used from 1868 to save on paper costs, and the mechanisation of the presses allowed newspapers to employ fewer skilled staff.

Provincial newspapers benefited from other technological developments in the late nineteenth century in the area of newsgathering. Railways were initially used to send copies of London newspapers, containing the latest national and foreign news, to the provinces but they were superseded by the electric telegraph. The advent of the telegraph in 1845, when the first message was transmitted to the *Morning Chronicle*, allowed the provincial press to receive foreign and national news speedily and cheaply. By 1854 the Intelligence Department of the Electric and International Telegraph Company was delivering political news, stock market information, and sports results to 120 provincial newspapers. International submarine telegraph cables began to link the

Brief History of Provincial Newspapers

Figure 3: Advertising in the *Wrexhamite*. Note the lack of illustrations and uniformity of text.

world: a permanent trans-Atlantic link was established in 1866, in 1872 the Madras–Australia link was established, and by 1880 nine telegraph cables crossed the Atlantic. In 1851 Julius Reuter, a naturalised German, established his international news agency in London, using this new technology. Although Reuter telegrams appeared in the *Manchester Guardian*, *Manchester Courier*, and *Liverpool Mercury* between May 1853 and December 1855, Reuter's business was primarily focused on the continent and the company did not secure subscriptions from leading London newspapers until late 1858 and early 1859. Within the UK, the Press Association (PA) was created in 1865 by provincial newspaper proprietors to ensure that no one newspaper or group of newspapers gained control of the telegraph system.

Another important change in the press in the nineteenth century, both national and provincial, was the arrival of 'New Journalism' in the 1880s. 'New Journalism' was pioneered by W. T. Stead at the *Pall Mall Gazette* which he began to edit in 1883. It emphasised novelty, variety, and sensationalism (as shown by features for women, sports columns, exposés, and illustrations) at the expense of more traditional news items such as parliamentary reports while foreign news became more concise.

The press had long been an important political instrument, both locally and nationally, and its importance greatly increased after the significant rise in the electorate following the 1867 Reform Act. The provincial press reported both local and national political news, especially at election time, and towards the end of the nineteenth century included news from a wide range of elected bodies such as the newly established School Boards and County Councils. Most early eighteenth-century provincial newspapers claimed to be neutral but by the Victorian era newspapers claiming allegiance to Liberalism or Conservatism were common. Many provincial newspapers were started with the financial support of local Liberals or Conservatives; the *Western Mail* founded by the 3rd Marquess of Bute and the *Wrexham Guardian* being examples.

By the beginning of the twentieth century, a national newspaper press was rising to challenge the provincial newspapers. In the mid-1850s the only 'national' newspaper was *The Times*, but improved rail communications allowed London newspapers to expand their circulation into the provinces. The *Daily Mail*, established in 1896, had a printing and distribution office in Manchester which allowed it to compete with daily morning newspapers in the north of England. As national newspapers began to expand further into the provinces, the number of provincial newspapers began to fall; the number of morning provincial newspapers in England fell from seventy in 1900 to forty-two in 1914; provincial evening newspapers fell from 101 to seventy-seven. Not only were provincial newspapers losing readers to the national press but also, crucially, advertising. Branded consumer goods needed to be nationally marketed to the largest possible audience, thereby depriving the provincial press of an important part of its advertising income.

In Wales
The history of the Welsh press differs from that of England because of the dual language nature of the country. Although Thomas Jones, a native of Corwen residing in Shrewsbury, may have produced the first Welsh-language newspaper in 1705, the first known newspaper to have been published in Wales was the Swansea-based English-language *Cambrian* in 1804. The late arrival of the Welsh press in comparison to the English can be explained by

poorer communications, a sparse, predominantly rural population, and, of course, the existence of two languages – Welsh being the language of the majority of the population. Poor communications meant not only that it was difficult to gather local news, but also that the arrival of London newspapers, containing the latest national and foreign news, may have been delayed, thus holding up the production of the newspaper. Similar delays could also affect the supply of stamped paper and therefore Welsh newspaper printers were obliged to keep excess supplies. Large towns near the border, which usually had a larger number of English-speakers than elsewhere in Wales, were served by English newspapers, for example Bristol, Gloucester, and Hereford newspapers circulated in Cardiff and Swansea, with Shrewsbury and Chester newspapers fulfilling a similar role for towns in North and Mid Wales.

The *Cambrian* was followed in 1808 by the *North Wales Gazette* (later the *North Wales Chronicle*) in Bangor, and the first Welsh-language newspaper, *Seren Gomer* [*Star of Gomer*] appeared in 1814. Like the *Cambrian*, *Seren Gomer* was published in Swansea, but unlike the English-language newspaper, it sought to be a national newspaper, circulating throughout Wales. Unfortunately, the newspaper ceased in August 1815 through a combination of the stamp duty, distribution problems, and lack of advertising. The first Welsh-language newspaper to run for a significant time (four years) was *Y Newyddiadur Hanesydd* [*The Historian's Newspaper*] (later *Chronicle yr Oes* [*Chronicle of the Ages*]) which ran from 1836 to 1840 and was published in Mold.

Although several Welsh-language newspapers were established after the reduction in stamp duty in 1836, few of them lasted for any significant length of time. Two noticeable exceptions were *Yr Amserau* [*The Times*], established in 1843 and *Yr Herald Cymraeg* [*The Welsh Herald*], established in 1855 – just before the abolition of stamp duty. *Yr Herald Cymraeg* was based in Caernarvon while *Yr Amserau* was initially published in Liverpool. These two newspapers merged to form *Baner ac Amserau Cymru* [*Banner and Times of Wales*], the dominant Welsh-language newspaper of the Victorian era, which was owned by the famous Denbigh-born printer and publisher Thomas Gee.

The English-language press was dominant in Wales. Between 1804 and 1855 forty-two newspapers appeared in south Wales, seven in the Welsh language, thirty-three in the English language, and two were bi-lingual. The daily Welsh press was limited to the south, specifically to English-language newspapers in Cardiff and Swansea. Swansea again produced a Welsh press 'first' with the arrival of the *Cambrian Daily Leader* in 1861 and by 1893 Swansea had a second morning daily, the *South Wales Daily Post*; both were priced at a halfpenny by 1900. Cardiff also had two daily newspapers; the *Western Mail*, established in 1869, and the *South Wales Daily News*, founded in 1872. The *Western Mail* has sought to become the main English-language newspaper in Wales but has yet to break the *Daily Post*'s hold on the north of the Principality.

By 1914 provincial newspapers had developed into important organs for the communication of ideas and news, both to their readers, and from their readers to government, and were an important service for the millions who lived outside London. They had faced repression and government attempts to control them, primarily by the 'taxes on knowledge', and became increasingly important political and commercial organs after 1855. Towards the end of the nineteenth century their influence began to wane, with improved railway links – which enabled London newspapers to reach the provinces more quickly – and the rise of the national press, as exemplified by the *Daily Mail*.

CHAPTER 3 – WREXHAM'S NEWSPAPERS

1. *Wrexham Recorder* [March 1848–January 1849]

Wrexham's first newspaper was a monthly twopenny, the *Wrexham Recorder*, which commenced publication in March 1848 and ran for eleven issues to January 1849. Physically it was more like a periodical and because it was published monthly it did not have to pay stamp duty. The *Recorder* was printed and published by its proprietor, Richard Hughes, at his General Printing Office in Church Street, Wrexham. Richard Hughes was the founder of the printing and publishing firm of Hughes & Son, which became one of the major publishers of Welsh-language books and music.

Figure 4: Richard Hughes.

Many modern day newspaper readers would not recognise the *Recorder* as it bore little resemblance to what would be considered a newspaper today. Over half of its content was made up of local news stories such as a report from the local Literary Association, and the December 1848 version was published as follows:

> We are happy to find, that excellent progress has been made in the establishment of the Literary Association. The room is attended every evening on which it is open by about fifty members, who seem very attentively engaged, either in perusing the periodicals with which the long table

is plentifully furnished, or in enjoying a quiet game of chess, which the Committee, in compliance with the wishes of a large body of the subscribers, have allowed to be introduced. Many parties have expressed a strong wish that newspapers should be purchased and supplied, but we believe the Committee have not made any arrangement for that purpose, though, we understand, many newspapers have been already given, and others promised, to be laid upon the table gratuitously. The Committee are at present, we believe, endeavouring to mature a plan for establishing classes. We hear too, that an arrangement has been made with a gentleman, well known as the author of several scientific treatises, to deliver an inaugural lecture early in January. Dr Hodgson of Manchester, formerly Secretary of the Mechanics' Institution, in Liverpool, has been prevented from doing so by the illness of his wife. The Committee have paid off some trifling incumbrances which were claimed upon the library formerly belonging to the Artizan's Library and Young Men's Society, and have taken possession of it, and as soon as it can be properly arranged it will be placed at the service of the members, who, we are informed, now reach 110 in number. We find on perusal of the rules of the Association, our fair readers may participate in its advantages, and for whose information we copy Rule 20: "Any lady on paying 10s. annually, shall receive a card entitling her to attend the lectures, and receive books from the library."

There was very little national news as its inclusion would have contravened the Stamp Act. The remainder of the newspaper consisted of feature-type articles which could be placed in type and printed well in advance of the printing deadline. Since there were no advertisements (possibly to avoid advertising duty) profits were dependent on sales. The

Recorder referred to itself as a periodical rather than a newspaper.

The *Recorder* lasted for less than a year. In its January 1849 issue the newspaper claimed that it was pleased with its current success and gave no indication that this would be the last issue to appear. The only indication of financial difficulty was a rise in price to threepence, possibly because it was losing its readers to the *Wrexham Registrar*.

Despite its brief existence, the role of the *Recorder* in the history of Wrexham newspapers should not be underestimated. It was the pioneer in its field and it is possible that its establishment encouraged the founding of the rival *Registrar*, the first in a line of important Wrexham newspapers. The *Recorder*'s publication in English by a predominantly Welsh-language printing and publishing firm reflected Wrexham society and culture in the early Victorian era. It is regrettable that the newspaper did not give any information as to its numerical and geographical circulation and expand upon its political views. The *Registrar* might have caused its demise, as its make-up was not sufficiently different from its cheaper rival.

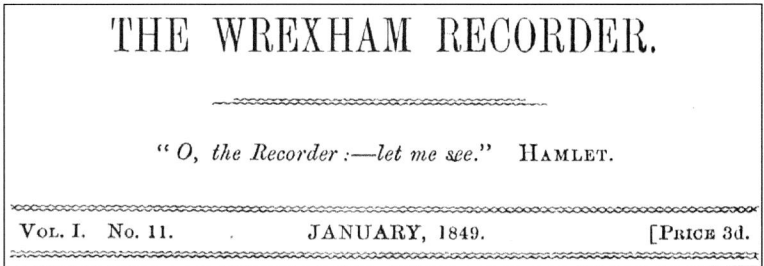

Figure 5: *Wrexham Recorder* masthead.

2. *Wrexham Registrar* [August 1848–December 1849]

The year 1848 also saw the founding of Wrexham's second newspaper, the *Wrexham Registrar and People's Friend* (*Wrexham Registrar*) by local printers William and George Bayley. The *Registrar* underwent several title changes and several breaks in publication but continued in one form or another until 1958 when it was incorporated into the *Wrexham Leader*. Without the *Registrar* and its success, Wrexham may have been deprived of its most important newspaper series.

Figure 6: George Bayley.

The first issue, published in August 1848, was very similar in format to the *Recorder* and consisted of sixteen double column pages. The pages were continuously numbered and contained very few advertisements. Priced at one penny, it was cheaper than its rival and ran for a total of seventeen issues. Its aims were set out in the first issue and included covering local events, promoting local sanitary, social and religious reforms with some entertaining and informative feature articles.

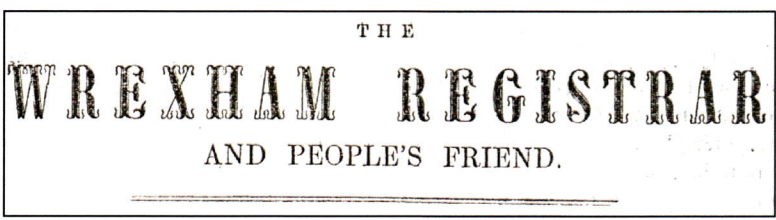

Figure 7: *Wrexham Registrar* masthead.

The *Registrar* predominantly contained essays and articles on local history but also included local, domestic, and foreign news. Readers were encouraged to send in their own contributions, for example, in the June 1849 issue, readers were requested to send in 'sketches of eminent men of the locality' which would form a series of articles. The second issue introduced a semi-editorial column which gave a brief résumé of the major events at home and overseas during the last month, often with some comment. For instance, the 'Retrospect of the Month' for Friday, December 1, 1848 covered the municipal elections, the death of Lord Melbourne, unrest in the Habsburg Austrian Empire, elections in France and the United States and the implications of the latter for the anti-slavery movement, while a separate article discussed 'The Lottery Mania'.

The *Registrar* was printed and published by its proprietors, brothers William and George Bayley at their General Printing Office in Hope Street, Wrexham. They were assisted by their brother Charles George, a china dealer and newsagent in Oswestry, who, like his brothers had been apprenticed to the printer Richard Hughes, founder of the *Wrexham Recorder*. Provincial newspapers of this time had low initial capital requirements and were often started and run as family businesses. In fact, several Bayley sons and grandsons were to become involved in the press trade. William Bayley founded his printing press in Wrexham around 1838 but by 1846 it was mainly run by George. They were keen to publish the newspaper

Figure 8: Charles George Bayley.

twice a month, but this enterprise would have to wait for another few years.

The March 1849 issue brought a change of title and size – the title was shortened to the *Wrexham Registrar* and its size reduced to twelve pages. Perhaps the termination of its local rival meant that the *Registrar* no longer felt the need to publish a sixteen-page newspaper when it could publish just twelve pages and still charge one penny.

Figure 9: Both Richard Hughes and George Bayley were buried in the Dissenters' Burial Ground in Rhosddu (now a public park). The obelisk is a memorial to Morgan Llwyd.

3. *Wrexham (Monthly) Advertiser* [January 1850– September 1852]

In January 1850 George Bayley launched a successor to the *Wrexham Registrar* – the *Wrexham Advertiser, and Register of Literary, Railway, Local and General Information*. It was a four-page penny monthly broadsheet, published on the first of each month and claiming a monthly circulation of 1,500 by

Wrexham's Newspapers

September 1852. It was unstamped, which was to cause legal difficulties for the proprietor.

Like the *Registrar* it included local, foreign and domestic news, Wrexham court cases, useful local information such as railway timetables, essays, historical information, poems and book reviews. The vast majority of the local news came from Wrexham. This suggests that either the circulation of the monthly newspaper was almost completely focused on Wrexham or that the newspaper was having difficulty in obtaining news from outside the town, as North Wales lacked an adequate transport system at this time. But unlike its predecessor, and as its name suggests, it contained advertisements.

However, by its third issue, the *Wrexham Advertiser* encountered a problem that was to trouble it throughout its existence. The editorial in this issue apologised for its late appearance and explained that the Commissioners of the Inland Revenue had decided that the newspaper must be stamped if it was to include local and national news. The newspaper proceeded to attack the stamp, advertising, and paper duties and hoped that they would soon be abolished so that Wrexham would be able to enjoy a weekly newspaper. Although the amount of local and national news was reduced in subsequent issues, a considerable amount of such information continued to appear, seemingly in defiance of the Commissioners.

In December 1850 the *Advertiser* announced that it would take the first step towards its owner's dream of a weekly newspaper for Wrexham and consequently, from January 1851 it would be published fortnightly on the first and fifteenth of each month. However, the *Wrexham Advertiser* survived for only four months as a fortnightly. No issue was published on 15 May and the next issue on the second of

June promised an explanation in the July issue as to why the *Wrexham Advertiser* had ceased fortnightly publication but no explanation was forthcoming. However, it is likely that it was once again connected with stamp duty. Partial confirmation appeared in January 1852 when the newspaper accused the Commissioners of the Inland Revenue of attempting to suppress all monthly periodicals which resembled newspapers in content or form. Without warning the *Wrexham Advertiser* ceased publication after thirty-seven issues in September 1852.

The monthly *Advertiser* was the first Wrexham newspaper to adopt a newspaper-like format, be produced in broadsheet form, and to include advertisements regularly. It printed more local, national, and foreign news than either of its two predecessors and set new standards for Wrexham newspapers. In addition by publishing fortnightly, albeit only briefly, the *Advertiser* signalled its owner's ambition of a weekly newspaper, and offers a case study of stamp duty and the Welsh press and the efforts made by the authorities to ensure that this tax was paid.

4.   *Wrexham (Weekly) Advertiser* [March 1854–1936]
The weekly version of the *Advertiser* was essentially a continuation of the monthly *Advertiser*, with a gap of a year and a half between the two newspapers. Weekly publication gave the newspaper a greater opportunity to serve the local community by reporting a wider range of news and political opinion. However the newspaper was now more expensive as it had to be stamped and this could have been the reason for initial sales being lower than those of the monthly version. Politically, it supported the Liberal party, with two of its owners becoming Liberal Mayors of Wrexham and

Oswestry respectively but was not as violent in its affections as its rival, the *Guardian* (see page 37).

The first issue of the weekly version of the *Advertiser* was scheduled to appear on 4 March 1854, but, in fact, it did not make its first appearance until a week later. It was priced at three pence, two pence more than its monthly predecessor. A third of this price was stamp duty which the newspaper was obliged to pay as a weekly publication. Stamp duty caused another difficulty as each issue had to be sent from Wrexham to Somerset House to be stamped. The four-page weekly was published on Saturday mornings with a second edition in the afternoon. In its first issue owner George Bayley stated that the main reason behind the establishment of the newspaper was the increasing importance of Denbighshire and Flintshire, and that they deserved a local newspaper to record events and to express local opinions.

Within a few years of its establishment, the newspaper had made several noticeable changes. Firstly, its price was reduced to two pence after the abolition of stamp duty in 1855. This led to an increase in circulation in early 1857 and the newspaper purchased a new steam printing machine which allowed it to produce 1,000 copies an hour. By 1858 the weekly *Advertiser* had exceeded the sales of the monthly version, selling 1,700 copies a week. As a consequence of mechanisation, in July 1861 it doubled its size to eight pages, enabling it to include more advertisements and also reflecting its increasing circulation, which reached nearly 3,000 a week by 1863.

Following the death of George Bayley (the newspaper's founder, proprietor, and editor) in January 1863, the newspaper came under the control of his widow Selina, his brother Charles George, and the new editor, George Bradley.

As Charles George lived in Oswestry, Bradley was presumably largely responsible for the daily running of the newspaper. Circulation increased after Bayley's death, supposedly because of sympathy for his family. George Bradley, Charles George Bayley, and Selina Bayley proceeded to establish the firm of Bayley & Bradley to carry out the printing of the newspaper. After the death of Bradley, control of the company seems to have moved away from the Bayley family to the children of Bradley, despite William Charles Bayley, son of George, editing the newspaper for over three years, before emigrating to South Africa in 1894.

Figure 10: George Bradley wearing his mayoral chain.

Several other changes were also made around this time. The newspaper offices moved from Hope Street to Bank Street in 1857, and then to the Music Hall in Henblas Street in 1868. A fourteen year lease was taken on the building and, when it expired, Bradley, Charles George Bayley, and Harry

Figure 11: Bradley Road, near Wrexham town centre was opened during George Bradley's time as Mayor of Wrexham (1881) and named in his honour.

Croom-Johnson (Bradley's son-in-law), took shares in the property. By 1870 the newspaper was claiming that it was read throughout Denbighshire and Flintshire, and also in parts of Merionethshire, Shropshire, and Cheshire. The *Advertiser* also took the opportunity to decide on a final title, having changed its subtitle every few years to reflect its circulation area and became the *Wrexham Advertiser and North Wales News*.

In April 1895 the *Advertiser* reduced its price to a penny (which made it the same price as the *Guardian*), in the hope of increasing its sales. In 1899 the *Advertiser* became connected to the national telephone exchange at Wrexham thus allowing reporters and advertisers to contact the newspaper more quickly. The newspaper was enlarged in February 1904 to give it more space for advertisements and news reports and this led to the introduction of a new column in September, the 'London Letter' being especially written for the newspaper and focusing on the action of Welsh MPs and important Welsh issues.

In 1907 a new editor, James Wright, (the replacement for John Rice Jones who had worked on the newspaper for fifteen years) brought several changes to the newspaper. One of the first changes he made was to alter the day of publication of the first edition from Friday to Thursday, the second edition remaining on Saturday. This change lasted less than a year as, despite a rise in circulation, the newspaper had received requests

Figure 12: John Rice Jones.

from both subscribers and advertisers to revert to the original day of publication. From 1909 the *Advertiser* produced a Mold edition and in March 1914 the newspaper expanded to twelve pages with the price remaining at one penny. The *Advertiser* remained at this size until September 1914 when it was reduced to its previous size of eight pages, probably because of incipient wartime paper shortages.

When it was established in 1854, the content of the weekly *Advertiser* was markedly different from that of its monthly predecessor. It contained far fewer features and more national news. Foreign news appeared regularly but its quantity depended on the prevailing international situation. The Crimean War was the first war to be covered in detail by the *Advertiser*, a war famed for the reporting of W.H. Russell of *The Times*. Other important years for war news were 1860 to 1865 for the American Civil War, 1870 for the Franco-Prussian War, and 1899–1902 for the Boer War, which saw the appearance of detailed reports on the actions of local soldiers in South Africa. The amount of national news fell over the years as improved transport links saw London newspapers appear in North Wales more frequently, thereby removing the need for a local newspaper to report national events. Foreign news was also affected and the *Advertiser* began to reflect a more local angle in its reporting.

A study of the *Advertiser*, as Wrexham's longest established newspaper, reflects a changing Wales and a changing Britain; socially, economically, politically, and culturally. Despite changes in society, the *Advertiser* remained loyal to the Liberal party, even after the party's influence waned after the end of the Lloyd George premiership. Its expansion in circulation and the establishment of publishing offices elsewhere in North East Wales and the border area strongly suggests that it was a successful and thriving newspaper, although there is evidence of a contraction in its area of influence in the early twentieth century. It is unfortunate that the newspaper did not give more detailed circulation and sales information as this may explain why no attempt was made to establish a daily or twice-weekly *Advertiser*. Whereas George Bayley was willing to take the risk of weekly publication, the syndicate that took control on his death may have been less willing to risk daily publication. Nevertheless, the *Advertiser* did show that it was possible to establish a prosperous weekly English-language newspaper in Wrexham.

5. *Wrexham Albion* [September–December 1854]

It is impossible to give a detailed history of the *Albion* for three main reasons. Firstly, it only ran for four issues and the first of these, which may have provided important information, has not survived. Secondly, its brief existence meant that it did not appear in any trade directories, and thirdly, the three surviving issues give very little information as to its origins, and political and religious viewpoints. It was a four-page A3 size newspaper, produced monthly, and priced at one penny. It was published in the middle of each month and so avoided paying stamp duty. The name of the newspaper's proprietor was not given, but it was printed and published by James Lindop at the Old Post Office on

Figure 13: James Lindop.

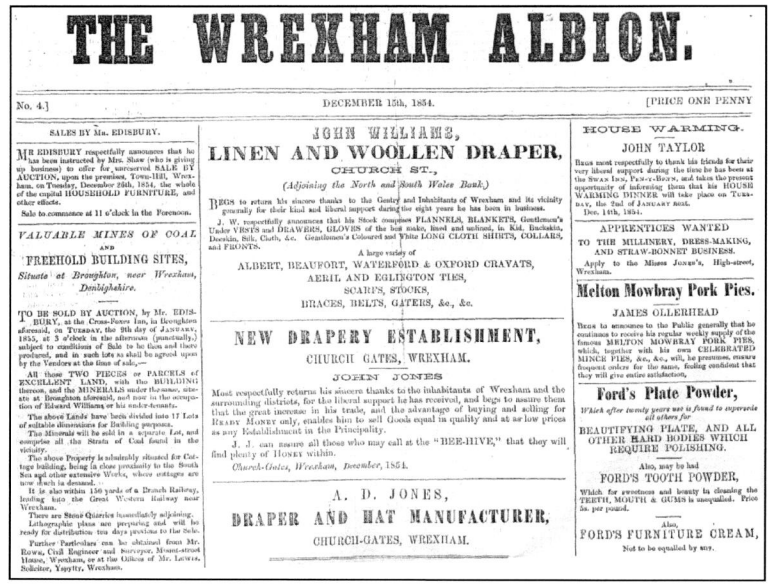

Figure 14: Extract from the front page of *The Wrexham Albion*.

Church Street. It seems highly probable that the *Albion* was the direct forerunner of the *Wrexhamite/Telegraph*. Both newspapers had the same printer and publisher in James Lindop, and the three surviving issues of the *Albion* each carry an advertisement for the *Wrexhamite*. According to an advertisement in its second issue, the first number of the *Wrexhamite* was due to be published on Wednesday, November 1, 1854 but it was not actually published until two months later. It is possible that the first issue of the *Albion* was so successful that its owner decided to convert it into a weekly newspaper, but this would have been a risk on the strength of one issue. Alternatively, the role of the *Albion* may have been to discover if there was a market for a second Wrexham newspaper.

6. *Wrexhamite* (*Wrexham Telegraph*) [January 1855–February 1867]

The *Wrexhamite* (later the *Wrexham Telegraph*) was the first Conservative newspaper published in Wrexham. It ran for twelve years and was owned by a series of proprietors. The first issue of the *Wrexhamite* was published on the second Thursday of January 1855, two months later than originally intended, under the title of the *Wrexhamite* and was priced at two pence.

The *Wrexhamite* failed to give any information about its ownership, the first issue merely stating that the newspaper was printed and published by James Lindop. *Mitchell's Press Directory* for 1856 gave Lindop as the newspaper's proprietor, but, as the *Advertiser* revealed, its actual owner was Wrexham solicitor and future Conservative Mayor, John Lewis. Unfortunately, the newspaper never explained why it felt it necessary to hide details relating to its ownership, although Lewis may have felt that newspaper proprietorship was not a suitable occupation for a solicitor and aspiring local politician. Lewis sold the newspaper in April 1858, having failed to be elected to Wrexham Town Council.

The last issue of 1855 announced that the newspaper would be enlarged to three times its size (later downgraded to twice) and would change its day of publication to Friday. It also altered its format from a four-page broadsheet to a small folio of sixteen pages. As with most newspapers of the time, the content focused primarily on politics, financial news, editorials, and foreign news. The political nature of the newspaper and its desire to support the Conservative party could account for the large amount of space devoted to editorials. A final change was the appointment of an unnamed new editor, described as someone who worked with London daily press, although the newspaper was still published by Lindop. As a result of this change, all the newspaper's general articles and news would be prepared in London. It is clear that the newspaper's new format was not popular, as a year later the *Wrexhamite* reverted to its original broadsheet form. In addition, the day of publication changed back to Thursday, possibly because publishing on a Friday placed it in direct competition with the *Advertiser*, whereas publishing on an earlier day may have given it an advantage over its rival. 1856 also saw the newspaper become embroiled in a libel case when Daniel Jones, a Wrexham cheese merchant, commenced an action against Lewis and Lindop. The *Wrexhamite* had published a small poem which Jones considered to be libellous. Lewis paid twenty shillings in damages plus costs and offered an apology.

Figure 15: Local food adverts in the *Wrexhamite*.

In January 1857 the newspaper changed its title from the *Wrexhamite* to the *Wrexham Telegraph and Denbighshire and Flintshire Reporter* in an attempt to appeal to readers outside Wrexham. It seems that the title change did greatly increase sales as four months later the newspaper was sold to a

Wrexham printer, Railton Potter. As a consequence of the sale, the newspaper's office moved from Lindop's printing office in Hope Street to Potter's in the High Street. Within a few months, at the end of 1858, Potter, claiming increasing pressure from his printing business, sold the newspaper to another printer, Charles Griffiths. The new owner promised that all attempts to improve the newspaper would be made and pledged his own involvement in the scheme. It seems that these attempts were successful as circulation reached 1,000 by July 1859. In 1859 the *Advertiser*'s former reporter, Richard Richards, was appointed editor. With the change in ownership came another change in location from High Street to Griffiths's General Printing Office at Bryn-y-Ffynon, then to Henblas Street in 1861, and High Street in January 1863. There was a further change of editor in January 1863 but the name of the new editor was not given. The newspaper appears to have suffered problems with some readers not paying their subscriptions and this could explain why the newspaper was sold in April 1863 to William Bellingham.

Bellingham made three important changes. The first change was the day of publication to Saturday, the second being an increase in size from four to eight pages, and the third was the newspaper's title from the *Wrexham Telegraph* to the *Denbighshire and Flintshire Telegraph, North Shropshire and West Cheshire Reporter*. From 1865 three editions of the *Telegraph* were published: on Wednesday morning, Thursday morning (special market edition for Wrexham only), and a Saturday edition published on Friday night and Saturday morning. This thrice-weekly newspaper was the closest Wrexham came to daily newspaper publication (before the weekday *Evening Leader* in 1973). Each issue was priced at one penny for four pages, the Saturday edition being expanded to eight pages from November 1866.

Naturally much of the news in the Wednesday edition was repeated in the Thursday and Saturday editions, and the existence of a special edition for Wrexham shows that, despite the newspaper's change in title, it still recognised the importance of Wrexham. In addition, the office was moved in April 1866 from Lambpit Street to Hope Chambers, Hope Street. The newspaper ceased in early 1867 but Bellingham gave no reason. The fact that the newspaper was not sold to another proprietor supports the belief that it was a commercial failure.

Figure 16: When the *Wrexham Telegraph* was owned by Railton Potter it was published at 18 High Street, now a public house.

As the first Conservative newspaper in Wrexham, the *Telegraph* showed that it was possible to establish a Conservative newspaper in North Wales (and have several Liberal supporters on the staff). If a newspaper's title was an accurate reflection of its geographical circulation area, then the *Telegraph* expanded its circulation from Wrexham into Denbighshire and Flintshire and then into north Shropshire and west Cheshire. It is especially regrettable that Bellingham declined to give any reasons for the cessation of the *Telegraph*, its abrupt ending suggesting that its statements of expanding geographical and numerical circulation were masking serious financial problems.

7. *Wrexham (North Wales) Guardian* [September 1869–1954]

On 4 September 1869, the first issue of the eight-page *Wrexham Guardian* was published from the *Guardian* Office, Bank Place. Its early years were insecure and the newspaper

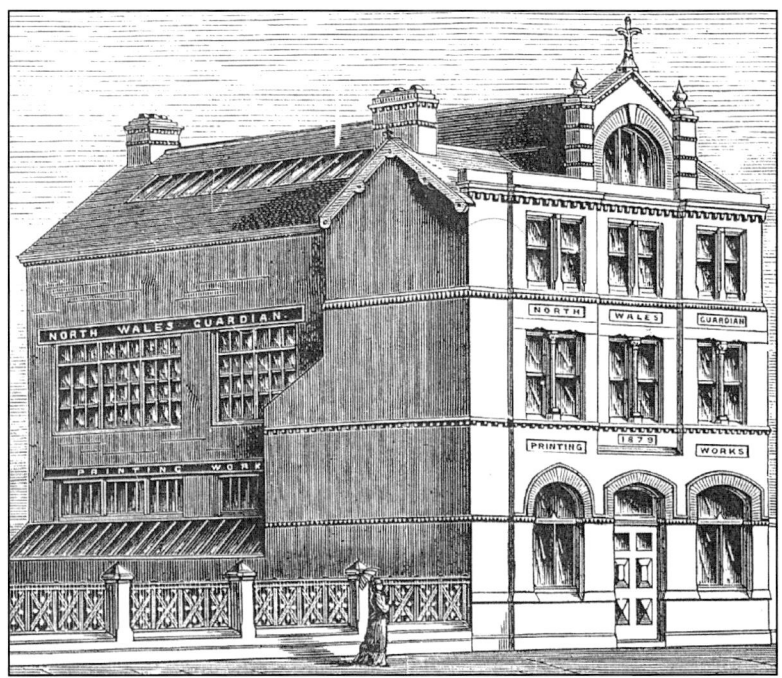

Figure 17: *North Wales Guardian* printing works.

came close to ending on several occasions as it suffered from substantial debts and its early survival was only made possible by a generous subsidy from its wealthy political backers. In addition, it suffered from a lack of internal stability as editors, managers and publishers changed with alarming frequency. In 1879 the newspaper gained a new owner and changed its name to the more geographically ambitious *North Wales Guardian* and this ushered in an era of stability and success.

The *Guardian* was owned by the North Wales Constitutional Press Company Limited and founded as a Conservative response to the Liberal victory in the 1868 general election to challenge the Liberal dominance of the North Wales press. The shareholders included some of the wealthiest Conservatives in North Wales – Sir Watkin Williams Wynn, the Hon. George Kenyon, Edmund Peel, Thomas Lloyd Fitzhugh, and Lord Edmund Hill-Trevor, three of whom (Sir Watkin, Kenyon, and Lord Edmund) were present or future MPs.

In 1873 the North Wales Constitutional Press Company was declared bankrupt. The *Guardian*'s average sales of just over 1,800 a week were significantly lower than those of the

Figure 18: Sir Watkin Williams Wynn.

Advertiser. However, in July it was able to secure a loan of £1,000 and that year's AGM passed a special resolution to increase the company's capital to £8,000 by issuing an additional 5,000 shares, which were unfortunately not purchased. It appears that the newspaper was surviving solely by a regular subsidy of approximately £1,000 a year from local Conservatives. Despite this, by April 1874 the company owed the bank £1,830 and the owner of the *North Wales Chronicle* made an offer for the *Wrexham Guardian*. A meeting was held in July to consider winding up the company and selling the newspaper but William Lee Brookes, a solicitor and Kenyon's election agent, loaned the company £1,000 (with interest at five per cent a year) which secured its short-term survival. Despite these financial difficulties, or maybe because of them, in April 1873 the Company founded another newspaper, the *Rhyl Guardian*, which duplicated much of the content found in its Wrexham counterpart. Between them the two newspapers circulated throughout North Wales and the border area.

The financial difficulties of the *Guardian* led to a rapid turnover of editors who usually fulfilled the multiple roles of printer, publisher, and manager. The first nine years saw seven different people at the helm of the *Guardian*: John Ramsden, John Vaughan, George William Spencer, Alfred Lloyd Row, Herman Behrens, William Garratt Jones, and John Hamlyn Lakeman. A measure of stability was achieved in June 1874 when Garratt Jones took over and remained editor until 1878. Naturally, each editor brought with him his own distinctive editorial style and such frequent changes must have been disconcerting for the readers.

Figure 19: John Ramsden, first editor of the *Wrexham Guardian*.

Politics, Publishing and Personalities

In the final months of its existence under the control of the North Wales Constitutional Press Company, the *Guardian* was involved in an unwelcome libel case. In November 1877, proceedings were initiated against the newspaper and William Garratt Jones, its printer and publisher. The newspaper had published an anonymous letter which referred to an inquest held by the Coroner for Denbighshire, Dr Evan Pierce, a notoriously prickly character, in the Denbigh Infirmary. The letter accused Dr Pierce of animosity against the infirmary and its staff and of relying on the opinion of his friend who had not treated the deceased. Garratt Jones offered an apology and paid costs (but stated that he believed the letter was true when he published it).

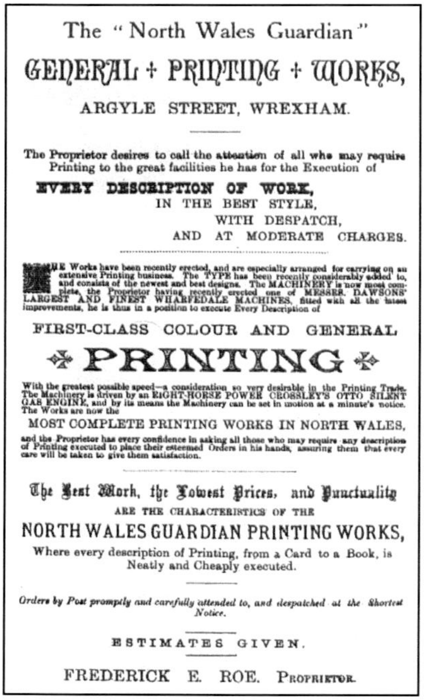

Figure 20: *North Wales Guardian* advertisement for printing services.

The *Guardian* continued to be beset by financial difficulties, and in 1878 Sir Watkin and Kenyon sent a printed circular to local Conservatives appealing for financial assistance. The *Guardian* now had a bank debt of £1,500; £500 would be required as working capital and the newspaper would need a subsidy of £300 a year. The printed circular detailed private donations that the company had received from its supporters and shareholders; Sir Watkin alone gave £2,870. Sir Watkin and Kenyon believed that the newspaper would be self-supporting within five years and stressed the importance of maintaining a Conservative newspaper in North Wales to fight the Liberal press. However, this appeal was unsuccessful and in August 1878 the newspaper, plant, and company were sold to the company secretary, Evan Morris, for £600 before being sold on to Frederick Edward Roe, the Dover-based printer and publisher of the *Dover Chronicle* and the *Kent and Sussex Advertiser*.

Figure 21: Sir Evan Morris.

Roe commenced his ownership of the *Guardian* with a dispute with its printers. He reduced wages from thirty-five to twenty-six shillings a week, decreased the number of staff, and complained that they did not do enough work. As a result of this cost-cutting measure he was able to reduce the price of the *Guardian* to a penny in 1885, thereby making it cheaper than its local rival, the *Advertiser*.

The *Guardian* was not the only Welsh newspaper owned by Roe. He also owned the *Rhyl Guardian* (established in 1873), both newspapers sharing the same publishing office in Rhyl. He was the founding proprietor of the *Shropshire and Montgomeryshire Post* (established in 1880) and from 1882 was the owner of *Y Dywysogaeth*, (established in 1870) the Welsh-language Church of England newspaper and moved its publication from Rhyl to Wrexham. The three English-language newspapers collaborated on advertising and on the

Figure 22: Griffith Parry Edwards.

collection of regional and national news. In September 1887 the *Guardian* was taken over by a new proprietor. The name of the new proprietor was never given but it was probably Evan Morris (later Sir Evan Morris, Mayor of Wrexham in 1888) the former company secretary of the North Wales Constitutional Press Company as, when the newspaper was next sold in February 1894, the sale was by the executors of his estate. In 1874 Morris had written to Kenyon offering to manage the *Guardian* himself and had bought it in 1878 before selling it to Roe. When the *Guardian* was sold in 1887, Frederick William Brodie became the new editor and manager. By 1890 the *Guardian* had new editors and managers in Joseph Henry White and Griffith Parry Edwards. White left in 1890, and when Edwards died suddenly in the *Guardian* office of a heart attack in February 1893 he was replaced by George Herbert Wykes, who stayed for less than a year.

In February 1894 the newspaper again changed hands, the title and the plant being sold to Messrs Jarman & Co., and the newspaper came under the control of Sydney Gardnor Jarman, a future Conservative Mayor of Wrexham who had been a reporter on the *Tiverton Gazette* and the *Bridgwater Mercury*, and a managing partner for the *Hunts County Gazette*. Sales were on average over 5,000 a week, but

Figure 23: Sydney Gardnor Jarman.

these were still lower than the *Advertiser*. The price was reduced to a halfpenny in April 1914 and when the First World War broke out, the newspaper immediately reduced its size to four pages.

The *Guardian*'s strong support for the Conservative party and Conservative politicians was frequently reflected in the newspaper's content and editorials. Gladstone and his politics were regularly attacked, but most venom was directed at the radical Liberal MPs for the Denbigh Boroughs and Denbighshire, Watkin Williams (Denbigh Boroughs 1868–1880) and George Osborne Morgan (Denbighshire 1868–1885, East Denbighshire 1885–1906) who were regularly criticised in the newspaper's editorials. Local Conservative politicians were lauded; in particular, George Kenyon (who contested the Denbigh Boroughs in 1874 and 1880, MP for the Denbigh Boroughs 1885–1895 and 1900–1906) and Sir Watkin Williams Wynn (MP for Denbighshire 1841–1885), two major early financial supporters of the newspaper. It also became more successful when it began to be run as a business, rather than as a mouthpiece for local Conservative politicians.

The *Guardian* is an example of a newspaper which endured difficult early years but eventually became a success. Its change of fortunes coincided with the replacement of the proprietary company with private individual ownership, thus implying that individual ownership was more successful than company ownership. The *Guardian* and its proprietors were also associated with at least three other Conservative newspapers in the area and it is possible that the establishment of the *Guardian* in 1869 may have been the beginning of a plan to establish a syndicate of Conservative newspapers across North Wales. The existence of the *Guardian* showed that it was possible for Wrexham to support two newspapers of different political persuasions, and it provided a rival for the *Advertiser*, thus challenging that newspaper's dominance of the Wrexham press.

8. *Wrexham Free Press* [February 1870–February 1873]

As the 'Free' in its title indicates, the *Free Press* was not created to promote a political viewpoint. Like the *Guardian* it was established by a company but outlived it. The *Free Press* was unique amongst Wrexham newspapers in that it metamorphosed into a temperance newspaper that aimed to circulate throughout Wales and England.

The *Free Press* was a short-lived, four-page, penny newspaper, published on Saturdays, which commenced in February 1870 and terminated three years later. It expanded to eight pages in October 1870 due to supposed pressure on space, but there was no simultaneous price rise. It was established by the Wrexham Free Press Newspaper Company which had been incorporated in January 1870 as a limited company, one of the shareholders being William Bayley (one of the founders of the *Registrar*). In its first issue the *Free Press* stated that the aim of the Company was to provide Wrexham and its neighbourhood with a cheap newspaper and to give local businesses the opportunity to advertise for a reasonable sum. This suggests that one of the main reasons for the establishment of the *Free Press* was to provide a vehicle of cheap advertising for Wrexham tradesmen and professionals.

The first printer and publisher of the *Free Press* was the Wrexham painter Gomer Jones who was also a shareholder in the company. It is unclear why a painter was chosen as opposed to one of the printers amongst the company's shareholders. No mention was made as to whether Jones was also the editor but by October he had been replaced by

W.H. Tilston. In June 1871 Alfred Raphael Gassion became the printer, publisher, sub-editor, reporter, and, as he claimed, *de facto* editor, of the newspaper and almost immediately commenced a feud with the newspaper's printers. He claimed that the printers, who were members of the Provincial Typographical Association, had 'thwarted him in several ways'. Gassion had attempted unsuccessfully to move the start of the printers' working day back to six o'clock instead of eight o'clock in the morning and had employed printers who were not members of the Provincial Typographical Association, thus causing the Association's printers to walk out.

When the *Free Press* was established it was clear from its title that both its content and circulation were going to concentrate primarily upon Wrexham. In addition, if the newspaper was established to advertise the wares of its shareholders, then, naturally, they would have concentrated on advertising their goods and services to the local population, especially as chemists and other similar professions did not usually attract clients from outside the locality. The Wrexham Free Press Newspaper Company stated that it aimed to supply Wrexham and the surrounding area and therefore it aimed to circulate predominantly in Wrexham and the local area, and did not, in the early days, aspire to cover Denbighshire and Flintshire, let alone the region of North Wales and the border area.

Although no information was given in the newspaper itself, the Wrexham Free Press Newspaper Company was officially wound up in September 1871, having stated that it could not continue its business due to its liabilities and it was sold for 'a three months bill' by the liquidator. This liquidation led to a series of disputes in the courts. In September a defaulting shareholder was forced to pay the £3 he owed to the company and two workmen successfully brought an action against the company's liquidator for a week's wages. One of the company's shareholders, Hugh Davies, became the temporary proprietor until the newspaper was sold to a new company in October 1871. Gassion left the company when it was sold but not before claiming that he had been urged by Hugh Davies to get rid of the members of the Provincial Typographical Association in order to pay lower wages. The new owners were not named, although there were rumours, later denied, that Thomas Gee, of *Y Faner*, was involved with the new company.

The time surrounding the newspaper's sale brought several other changes besides ownership to the *Free Press*. In September 1871, the *Free Press* changed its subtitle to the *North Wales Advertiser* which reflected a more regional character, although, unlike the *Wrexham Advertiser* and the *Wrexham Guardian*, it did not include either Cheshire or Shropshire in its subtitle. Gassion was replaced in November 1871 by David Hamer. Gassion and Hamer had a tempestuous relationship: Gassion accused Hamer of threatening language and saying that he (Hamer) would 'kick him out of the window', and consequently Hamer was bound over to keep the peace for six months on his own recognisance of £5. It also appeared that Hamer too, had difficulties in producing the newspaper and the workforce was no more amenable to him than Gassion.

In 1872 the title was changed to the *Wrexham Free Press, Mold and Holywell Journal* as the newspaper may have decided to expand to local towns without their own newspaper that were a reasonable distance from Wrexham. Sometime in 1872 James Jones became the new printer and publisher and the newspaper's editor at this time was William Lester, who, as a local temperance campaigner, may have been instrumental in the next major change for the newspaper.

In February 1873 an editorial announced that the *Free Press* would be converted into a temperance newspaper under the title of the *Good Templar Advocate and General Intelligencer*. Establishing a temperance newspaper in Wrexham, a town well known for its brewing industry, seemed a somewhat futile gesture. Four of the company shareholders were involved in the alcohol trade, one of whom, Peter Walker (local brewer and Conservative Mayor of Wrexham), held fifty shares. Walker was also one of the directors of the North Wales Constitutional Press Company and a shareholder in the Wrexham Free Press Company. In the early statements to readers, no mention had been made of promoting the temperance cause and, indeed, the newspaper appeared to have abhorred those members of the press who promoted the views of a clique as much as those promoting the views of a political party. Despite this, there are indications that the *Free Press* was sympathetic to the temperance cause, for example, in 1871 it published editorials attacking the Licensing Bill and several members of its staff, who were temperance advocates, most notably former printer and publisher Gomer Jones who ran a temperance hotel and managers W.H. Tilston and William Lester who were both members of the pro-temperance UK Alliance. The *Free Press* claimed that its promotion of the temperance cause had resulted in the

Figure 24: Peter Walker's obelisk in Ruthin Road Cemetery.

loss of support from some sixty publican subscribers and this seems at odds with its policy of continuing to accept alcohol advertisements. To compensate for the loss of support from publicans, the *Free Press* claimed that increased working-class subscriptions had led to sales more than doubling to 4,000 a week.

The *Good Templar Advocate and General Intelligencer* was not a success. It may have been a successor to the *Wrexham Temperance Messenger* which ran for only one issue in January 1873. The newspaper's new owners, the International Order of Good Templars, were clearly expecting the new newspaper to be a success. The newspaper anticipated a circulation of at least 6,000 and for it to be read in over 300 Good Templar Lodges. Despite these claims, the *Intelligencer* was a failure, changing its name to the *Templar of Wales* in May 1873 before ceasing in September that year. Brewing, it appeared, had more supporters in Wrexham than the Good Templars.

The existence of the *Free Press* strongly suggests that there may have been sufficient readers to justify the existence of a daily newspaper in Wrexham as the town was able to support three newspapers (although it appears that the *Guardian* was initially supported more by the Conservative party than the people of Wrexham) for three years. Its metamorphosis into a temperance newspaper was an interesting occurrence and its statement that its circulation had arisen as a result of its adoption of the temperance cause poses the question as to why the *Free Press* was then unable to transform itself successfully into a temperance propaganda tool. It is unfortunate that more information as to the proprietorship of the newspaper after the disbanding of the Wrexham Free Press Company is not available. Perhaps the main conclusions to be drawn from the *Free Press* are that

Wrexham newspapers which were organised by a company and those supporting the temperance cause were unsuccessful in Wrexham.

9. *The Illustrated Wrexham Argus and North Wales Athlete* [August 1884–December 1916]

In many respects, the *Argus* harked back to the early years of press publishing in Wrexham with its journal-like format, heavy dependence on feature articles, and its monthly appearance. It could be said that the *Argus* was not a monthly newspaper, but instead a journal containing some local news. Its first issue appeared in August 1884, having been printed, interestingly, next to the room which saw the production of the first issue of the *Advertiser* – considered a fortunate omen by its editor. Around a quarter to a third of its sixteen pages were taken up with local news and sport, the majority of the newspaper being devoted to short stories and features. There was a separate section of sports news, titled *North Wales Athlete*, which covered football, cricket, bowling, cycling, and other pastimes. It expanded by four pages in April 1885, claiming a need for extra advertising space. Its editor throughout its entire existence was William Arthur Berkley, who also worked as a correspondent for several Liverpool newspapers.

As expected for a newspaper circulating in a medium-sized town with two established local rivals, the *Argus* was always keen to stress its qualities to potential advertisers. By 1900 it was pleased to announce that it was taken as far away as London in the City News Rooms, the British & Colonial News Rooms, and the Central Agency, and in Bristol in Jones Brothers. Despite being read in such locations, the *Argus* remained a strong advocate of Wrexham and appeared to be content to focus on the town to the exclusion of anywhere else in North Wales.

As was the case with many other newspapers, the *Argus* was brought to an end by the First World War. In 1915 it appeared sporadically – only three times in the first seven months – and its only appearance after June 1916 was its last issue in December of that year. There was no indication that this was to be the last issue and the newspaper continued to appear in the listing in *Mitchell's Press Directory* for several years after.

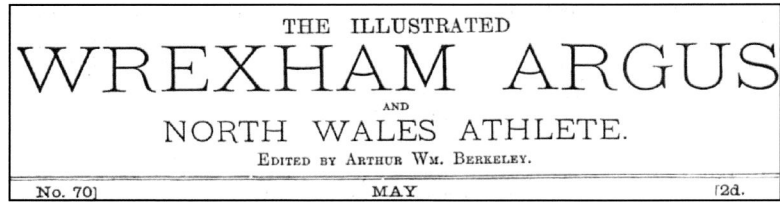

Figure 25: *Wrexham Argus* masthead.

Wrexham is fortunate in being one of the few towns in North Wales to be able to boast the appearance of a newspaper before the abolition of the Stamp Act and its press offers a varied sample in terms of time, longevity, political and religious views, and success or failure. With at least two, and sometimes three, newspapers existing for most of the years between 1848 and 1914, rivalry was keen and sometimes broke out into vicious insults and redress to the law.

CHAPTER 4 – INTER-NEWSPAPER RIVALRY

Inter-newspaper rivalry was very much a staple of the press trade. While opposing political and religious viewpoints caused friction between newspapers, sometimes rivalry was little more than a desire to entice readers away from rivals to boost readership and sales.

Recorder and *Registrar*
The rivalry between the *Recorder* and *Registrar* conducted at the outset of Wrexham's press history appeared to be extremely civilised. The *Recorder* never publicly commented on its rival and by the time the *Registrar* did comment critically upon its rival the *Recorder* had ceased to exist so its attack was largely immaterial.

Advertiser and *Telegraph*
If the rivalry between the *Recorder* and *Registrar* was conducted largely away from each newspaper's columns, this cannot be said for the *Advertiser* and *Telegraph*, whose intense rivalry was in no small part due to their promotion of different political parties. Within a few weeks of its launch, the *Telegraph* attacked its rival for claiming to be the only weekly newspaper in Denbighshire, followed a month later by claims that the *Advertiser* was making an unnecessary fuss when its reporter was excluded from the courts. In contrast, when the *Telegraph*'s own representative was excluded from Wrexham Town Council meetings in 1857, the Liberals were promptly blamed. The feud intensified in late 1856 when the *Advertiser* claimed that Wrexham solicitor John Lewis was the *Telegraph*'s hitherto unknown proprietor when it published that newspaper's declaration of ownership, casting aspersions as to why the solicitor had

failed to acknowledge his ownership openly. In return the *Telegraph* claimed that its ownership was well known.

In 1857 the feud moved on to the courts. The background to the case was complex but began with an article published in the *Advertiser* in May 1856 which accused the Vicar of Ruabon of breaking into an old chest in the parish church and removing some of the documents for an unspecified reason. When the newspaper discovered that some of this information, supplied by a reader, was only partially correct, it inserted two retractions. A month later an anonymous letter appeared in the *Telegraph* urging the Vicar to sue for libel. When he did so, he employed John Lewis as his solicitor. The *Advertiser* suggested that Lewis himself either wrote the letter, or, at least, sanctioned its insertion, and insulted him as selfish and unprofessional. Lewis promptly sued for £100, but the jury awarded only £10. George Bayley's supporters collected £191 to defray the £10 award and the costs of the case. The *Advertiser* believed that Lewis took action in retaliation for its publicising of Daniel Jones's libel case against the *Telegraph*.

The ongoing dispute between the two newspapers did not terminate with the libel trial. In February 1858 the *Telegraph* accused the *Advertiser* of plagiarising its mining news (although the *Advertiser* was not the only newspaper to be so accused). The *Telegraph* also attempted to humiliate its rival in the affair of its ex-editor Richard Richards. After the *Advertiser* had dismissed Richards (whom it described as a reporter), he wrote to the *Telegraph* stating that he had, in fact, been its editor and that his duties generally consisted of merely cutting and pasting news from other newspapers including the *Telegraph*. This letter may have led to Richards securing the position of *Telegraph* editor. The attacks continued throughout 1859 and 1860, perhaps inspired by Richards who sought to humiliate his previous employer.

In 1859 the *Advertiser* cast doubt upon the success of the *Telegraph* when it stated that it was near to closure and its reports were frequently incorrect. Furthermore, it implied that the *Telegraph* was financially supported by the Conservative party. In June 1861 the *Telegraph* published an anonymous letter accusing the *Advertiser* of deliberately misstating facts in an attempt to damage the Conservative party in the Town Council and a month later another anonymous letter writer described the *Advertiser* as a hypocrite that lacked the courage to express its own views for fear of losing readers and advertisements.

In 1864 the *Advertiser* and the *Telegraph* became engaged in dispute over each other's circulation. The *Advertiser* reiterated that it had the highest circulation of all North Wales newspapers and challenged the *Telegraph* to submit its books to a third party and the *Advertiser* would do the same. It would also allow the third party to see the newspapers being printed for a month and meet agents in order to establish the number of unsold copies. The third party would then judge which newspaper had the higher circulation, with the loser paying all expenses and donating £5 to the Denbigh Lunatic Asylum. There is no evidence that this challenge was ever accepted. The takeover by William Bellingham in 1865 brought an end, at least in newspaper columns, to the rivalry.

Advertiser, *Shrewsbury Chronicle* and *Chester Courant*
In late 1868 the *Shrewsbury Chronicle* and the *Chester Courant* published newspaper sales figures for newspapers published in North Wales, Shropshire, and Cheshire based on the number of stamps issued to each newspaper. By this time

newspapers bought stamps only for postage and unlike pre-1855 stamps, the number purchased did not accurately indicate sales. The *Advertiser* was not on the list. It immediately attacked the statistics as incomplete, incorrect and out of date. It was important for the *Advertiser* to act quickly to condemn the figures, as advertisers might have ceased to advertise in the *Advertiser* if they believed it to have low sales figures.

Advertiser and *Guardian*

If the rivalry between the *Advertiser* and the *Telegraph* was unpleasant and nasty, that between the *Advertiser* and the *Guardian* was even more vitriolic. Surprisingly, it took nearly a year for the rivalry to begin; the *Advertiser* was accused of whining pathetically when it lost the county advertisements for Flintshire to the *Guardian*. It was also charged with editorial boastfulness and exaggeration, and of fabricating correspondents' letters. This was merely the beginning of an intense rivalry between two newspapers of contrasting political and religious viewpoints, which were both seeking regional influence and circulation.

In 1878 perhaps the greatest scoop in Wrexham newspaper history was unearthed by the *Advertiser* and dealt a damaging blow to its rival. With the aid of Watkin Williams, the Liberal MP for the Denbigh Boroughs, the *Advertiser* was able to reveal the names of the financial supporters of the North Wales Constitutional Press Company, the body which owned the *Guardian*. The *Advertiser* published a printed circular dated 24 January 1878 which it had received from Williams, written by local Conservatives Sir Watkin Williams Wynn and George Kenyon, appealing for money for the *Guardian*, and listing the names of those who had financially supported the newspaper over the past eight years. The *Advertiser* must have been pleased to publicise Williams's view that the *Guardian* had failed to secure sufficient support and that it was dishonest for a newspaper to exist by private financial support rather than commercial success. The *Advertiser* added that, in its opinion, it was immoral for a newspaper, financially supported by a political party, to pass itself off as one advocating and responding to public opinion and was concerned that the views of such a print would be believed by those who did not know that it was subsidised, namely the poor and uneducated. Therefore the *Advertiser* could argue that it was assisting the public, by making them aware of the financial status of the *Guardian*, and its implication that the newspaper would be unable to survive without its subsidy from its wealthy Conservative backers was obviously aimed at hastening the *Guardian*'s demise.

This rivalry continued throughout the years. An 1880 *Guardian* editorial criticised the *Advertiser*'s quality of journalism. Anonymous letters, allegedly from satisfied readers, appeared in the *Guardian* commending it for offering a welcome alternative to the Liberal newspapers of North Wales.

After the winding-up of the North Wales Constitutional Press Company and the sale of the *Guardian* such attacks declined in frequency, possibly because the new owner was running the newspaper as a commercial rather than a political enterprise. When attacks were published, it was usually because the *Guardian* believed that itself or the Conservative party had been misrepresented in some way. In 1885 it condemned the *Advertiser* for falsely stating that Wrexham's Conservatives were planning to establish an Orangemen's Association, and also in December 1891 for stating that Kenyon would be opposed as the Conservative candidate for the Denbigh Boroughs at the next election.

Guardian and *Oswestry Advertiser*

Within two months of its first appearance, the *Guardian* attacked the *Oswestry Advertizer* for failing to provide sufficiently accurate information in its reporting of an annual stag hunt dinner. The *Oswestry Advertizer*'s retort to this was met with a complaint from the *Wrexham Guardian* that it (*Oswestry Advertizer*) either sulked or indulged in convoluted language when criticised. In the same month, the *Oswestry Advertizer*'s lapse in publishing a forged letter supposedly from Sir Watkin Williams Wynn stating that he intended to address his constituents next month, allowed the *Guardian* to accuse the Liberal newspaper of credulity and disseminating a false report. After this episode, no further comment was made upon the Oswestry newspaper. Attacks upon this Liberal rival may have been continued by the *Shropshire and Montgomeryshire Post* which had a more direct local rivalry with the *Oswestry Advertizer*.

Advertiser, *Guardian* and *Carnarvon Herald*

Considering the rivalry between Wrexham's newspapers, it is perhaps surprising that in January 1877 reporters from the *Guardian*, *Advertiser* and the *Chester Chronicle* joined forces to complain about the tactics of the *Carnarvon Herald* and its reporters. A reporter for the *Carnarvon Herald* was accused of taking the only copy of a list of bridal presents and immediately sending it to his editor, depriving his fellow reporters of its contents while knowing that they wished to see the list. That such a trivial incident caused such a reaction suggests keen competition amongst the newspapers of North Wales and that survival and success were more important than politics.

Two years later the *Carnarvon Herald* again angered the *Guardian*. A report in the *Carnarvon Herald* stated the only reason that the *Guardian* was found in the major hotels of North Wales was that it was given to them free of charge. It is possible that some of these 'major hotels' were located in places such as Llandudno, Bangor, Holyhead and Caernarvon which were all within the *Carnarvon Herald*'s main catchment area, thus making competitive rivalry the reason behind the statement. Roe promptly wrote a letter of protest to Evans, the editor of the *Carnarvon Herald*, stating that the statement was untrue and designed to cause financial damage to himself and his newspaper. The *Carnarvon Herald* consequently issued a correction.

Free Press, *Advertiser* and *Guardian*
In its first issue, the *Free Press* stated its disapproval of party newspapers, but did not specifically mention its local rivals, the Liberal *Advertiser* and the Conservative *Guardian*. The newspaper was, no doubt, attempting to adhere to its stated policy of excluding personal comments from its pages. Despite this sentiment, both newspapers were attacked, but because of their alleged inferiority to the *Free Press* rather than their political views: in April 1871 the *Free Press* claimed that the *Guardian*'s news was a fortnight behind its own and that it was published slightly earlier than the *Advertiser*.

The *Argus*, *Advertiser* and *Guardian*
Perhaps it was a show of independence, a desire to prove that it was not afraid of its more established local rivals that led to the *Argus* attacking both the *Advertiser* and the *Guardian*. In less than a year after its establishment the *Argus*

had accused both newspapers of plagiarising its reports, gleefully criticising factual errors in the *Advertiser,* and describing the *Guardian* as a blunderer. The accusations may have been propelled by the need for the newspaper to establish itself and distinguish itself from the Liberal and Conservative party newspapers. After this early flurry of comments, the *Argus* generally refrained from criticising its rivals and focused on its own virtues.

Multiple newspapers with different political opinions were a recipe for jibes and insults between different titles. The rivalry between Wrexham's newspapers was rarely polite and civilised, usually offensive and brutal. Perhaps it is surprising that there were not more cases of recourse to the law of libel when considering some of the statements made, although the case of the *Advertiser* and the Vicar of Ruabon could have discouraged this. Eventually, such vitriolic comments died out; maybe owners and editors realised that improving one's own newspaper would gain more readers that attacking one's rivals.

CONCLUSION

Up until the First World War, two newspapers dominated the Wrexham newspaper market – the *Advertiser* and the *Guardian*. Which one could claim to be the more successful title? In terms of revenue and circulation figures it would be the *Advertiser* – having grown from humble beginnings as the *Wrexham Registrar* to become Wrexham's first weekly newspaper and surviving, albeit with breaks in its circulation, for over a century. The *Guardian* survived for eighty-five years as the flag bearer for Conservatism in Liberal- and later Labour-dominated, North East Wales. That in itself is an impressive tale of survival and, in addition, it was able to claim a far wider geographical circulation than the *Advertiser*, possessing agents in and reporting news from throughout North Wales. This was probably due to its political leanings, as it would have needed to circulate over a far wider geographical area to reach its Conservative supporters. If any Wrexham newspaper could claim regional (i.e. North Wales) influence, it would be the *Guardian*. Surrounding these two giants were a number of smaller, shorter-lived newspapers that each contributed to Wrexham's press history. The *Recorder* demonstrated that there was the market and desire for a newspaper in Wrexham, the *Albion* showed that a market existed for a Conservative newspaper, the *Telegraph* indicated that Wrexham could support two competing newspapers, and the *Free Press* suggested that the tradesmen of Wrexham believed that they were not being well served by the *Advertiser* and *Guardian*, so set up their own newspaper.

EPILOGUE

The First World War brought massive upheaval to Wrexham life and delayed the appearance of a significant new arrival in the Wrexham newspaper field. The *Wrexham Leader* – owned by Woodall, Minshall & Thomas, the owners of the *Oswestry & Border Counties Advertizer* – was originally intended to appear in 1914 but due to wartime paper shortage finally arrived in 1920. It was printed at the Caxton Press in Oswestry and published at the Border Press in Wrexham. This dual-location system meant in practice that the editorial work and news-gathering was done in Wrexham and the actual printing of the newspaper took place in Oswestry, with the newspaper being then sent to Wrexham for sale. The *Leader*'s aim was to produce an up-to-date newspaper which would report news from the Wrexham area but would not support any political party or particular interest. Its first editor was the Oswestry–born journalist, George Lerry, MBE who had been the junior reporter covering Wrexham for the *Oswestry & Border Counties Advertizer* since 1903, aged just twenty. Lerry was to remain editor until 1948 and was to become a well-known local figure.

The *Leader* came to eclipse both the *Advertiser* and the *Guardian*. In 1921 Woodall, Minshall & Thomas purchased the important Welsh-language publishers Hughes & Son, whose founder Richard Hughes published Wrexham's first newspaper back in 1848. By 1930, the *Leader*'s circulation had reached 16,500 a week, a rise of over 11,000 since its first issue. In 1933 Bayley & Bradley, the owner of the *Advertiser*, was sold to Roland Thomas (of Woodall, Minshall & Thomas) and the directors of the *Leader*. In 1936 Woodall, Minshall & Thomas purchased the *Wrexham Star* (established 1934) and

Epilogue

merged the *Advertiser* and *Star* to create the tabloid-like *Wrexham Advertiser & Star*. The *Advertiser & Star* ceased publication in December 1945, only to re-start in April 1953, finally ending in 1957 when the *Leader* switched to twice-weekly production, taking the *Advertiser & Star*'s Tuesday slot. The *Guardian* continued until 1954. On his retirement, Percy Jarman (son of Sydney, who purchased the newspaper in 1894) was unable to find anyone to continue the newspaper. An era ended, leaving the *Leader* dominant in the Wrexham weekly newspaper market.

The *Wrexham Leader* was joined by a weekday daily newspaper from the same stable in October 1973 when the *Wrexham Evening Leader* arrived. The *Evening Leader* later expanded to include Flintshire and Chester variants. In 2009 it switched to morning production, changing its title to the *Leader*. In becoming Wrexham's first daily weekday morning newspaper, the *Leader* was breaking new ground. It will be interesting to discover, in a few years time, whether or not this change has been successful. In response to this change, the Trinity Mirror-owned *Daily Post* split its popular North Wales edition into separate editions for North East and North West Wales in January 2011. It will certainly be interesting to see if North East Wales can support two daily morning titles or whether the *Leader* will revert back to evening publication. The *Wrexham Leader* still continues, although it has been free of charge since 1993.

Wrexham has followed the trend towards large newspaper conglomerates owning several titles. In 1965, the *Chester Chronicle* became part of Thomson Regional Newspapers and is now part of Trinity Mirror, who own over 240 national and regional newspapers, including the *Daily Post*. Today, Woodall, Minshall & Thomas are known as North Wales Newspapers and publish the *Oswestry & Border Counties*

Figure 26: Advertising the new *Daily Post* editions on local buses in February 2011.

Advertizer, Whitchurch Herald, North Wales Pioneer, Y Cymro, Denbighshire Free Press, County Times and Express, North Wales Chronicle, Rhyl, Prestatyn and Abergele Journal and *Flintshire Standard,* in addition to the *Wrexham Leader* and weekday daily the *Leader* (previously the *Evening Leader*). It remains difficult for a new title to break into a local newspaper market. The *Wrexham Gazette* lasted for less than six years between 1967 and 1973, while the Trinity Mirror-backed *Wrexham Mail* (1988–2008) and its successor, the very short-lived *Wrexham Chronicle*, were free weekly newspapers.

The Victorian era has been recognised as the 'golden age' of the provincial press, most notably by Frank Manders and Maurice Milne in their respective studies of the press in North East England. As the only source of news for much of the population, the provincial press wielded significant influence and newspapers were founded for their political influence as much as for their business benefits. By the beginning of the twentieth century a national newspaper press was rising to

Epilogue

challenge the provincial newspapers. In the mid-1850s the only 'national' newspaper was the *Times*, but improved rail communications allowed London newspapers to expand their circulation into the provinces. The *Daily Mail*, established in 1896, had a printing and distribution office in Manchester which allowed it to compete with daily morning newspapers in the north of England. As national newspapers began to expand further into the provinces, the number of provincial newspapers began to fall, especially amongst provincial morning dailies. Not only were provincial newspapers losing readers to the national press but also, crucially, branded national advertising. The rise of large conglomerates like North Wales Newspapers and Trinity Mirror ensured the survival of many provincial newspapers in the twentieth century, and we wait to see how the provincial press deals with challenges such as the internet and financial instability into the twenty-first century. As a result, this period between 1848 and 1914 could well be seen in retrospect as the 'golden age' of newspaper publishing in the Wrexham area.

APPENDIX

Advertiser editors
1850–1863	George Bayley
1863–1890	George Bradley
1890–1894	William Charles Bayley
1894–1895	Possibly Frederic Bowser Mason
1896–1907	John Rice Jones
1907–1927	James Wright
1927–?	J.G. Benson

Wrexhamite/Telegraph owners
1855–1858	John Lewis
1858	Railton Potter
1858–1863	Charles Griffiths
1863–1867	William Bellingham

Printers and publishers (probably also editors) of *Wrexham Guardian*
1869–1870	John Ramsden
1870–1872	John Vaughan
1872–1873	George William Spencer
1873	Alfred Lloyd Row
1874	Herman Behrens
1874–1878	William Garratt Jones
1878	John Hamlyn Lakeman
1878–1887	Frederick Edward Roe
1887–1890	Frederick William Brodie
1890	Joseph Henry White & Griffith Parry Edwards (joint)

Appendix

1890–1893	Griffith Parry Edwards
1893–1894	George Herbert Wykes
1894–	Sydney Gardnor Jarman, who was followed by his son Percy, who edited the *Guardian* until his retirement in 1954 when the newspaper ceased.

***Free Press* editors**

1869	Possibly Gomer Jones
1870	W.H. Tilston
1870	Alfred Raphael Gassion
1871	David Hamer
1872–1873	William Lester

SELECTED BIBLIOGRAPHY

Aspinall, A. *Politics and the Press, c.1780–1850*. London: Home and Van Thal, 1949.

Baughan, Peter E. *The Chester and Holyhead Railway*, 2nd edn. Newton Abbot: David & Charles, 1972.

Baughan, Peter E. *A Regional History of the Railways of Great Britain: Volume 11 North and Mid Wales*, 2nd edn. Nairn: David St John Thomas, 1991.

Boyce, George, Curran, James and Wingate, Pauline (Eds). *Newspaper History from the Seventeenth Century to the Present Day*. London: Constable and Company, 1978.

Boyd, James I.C. *The Wrexham, Mold & Connah's Quay Railway: including the Buckley Railway*. Oxford: Oakwood, 1991.

Brake, Laurel, Jones, Aled and Madden, Lionel. *Investigating Victorian Journalism*. Basingstoke: Macmillan, 1990.

Brown, Lucy. *Victorian News and Newspapers*. Oxford: Clarendon, 1985.

Christiansen, Rex. *Forgotten Railways: North and Mid Wales*. Newton Abbot: David & Charles, 1970.

Cranfield, G.A. *The Development of the Provincial Newspaper, 1700–1760*. Oxford: Clarendon, 1964.

Selected Bibliography

Rees, R.D. 'A History of South Wales Newspapers to 1855'. MA Thesis, University of Reading, 1954.

Shattock, Joanne and Wolff, Michael (Eds). *The Victorian Periodical Press: samplings and soundings*. Leicester: Leicester University Press, 1982.

Thomas, Robbie. *The Advertizer Family: a history of North Wales Newspapers Limited*. Oswestry: North Wales Newspapers, 1988.

Wicklam, S.I. 'The Growth and Development of Printing in the Wrexham Area'. *Denbighshire Historical Society Transactions*, 35 (1986): 39–60.

Wiles, R.M. *Freshest Advices: early provincial newspapers in England*. Columbus: Ohio State University Press, 1965.

Williams, John. *Digest of Welsh Historical Statistics*. 2 vols. Cardiff: The Welsh Office, 1985.

Williams, W. Alister. *The Encyclopaedia of Wrexham*. rev. edn. Wrexham: Bridge Books, 2010.

Manuscript Sources
Flintshire Record Office. D/KT/22. Papers of the Hon. George Kenyon: records and correspondence of North Wales Constitutional Press Company Limited.

The National Archives, BT31/1508/4705. Records of Wrexham Free Press Newspaper Company.

The National Archives, BT31/1552/4989. Records of North Wales Constitutional Press Company Limited.

National Library of Wales. History of the Wrexham Printers' Society from 1818 to 1893, Facs. 695.

University of Warwick, Modern Records Centre. Provincial Typographical Association, MSS 39A/TA/7/DEP/1. Records on F.E. Roe's management of the *Wrexham Guardian*.

University of Warwick, Modern Records Centre. Provincial Typographical Association, MSS 39A/TA/1/8. Records on A.R. Gassion's management of the *Wrexham Free Press*.

Wrexham Museum, Notes on History of *Wrexham Advertiser* compiled by Elizabeth Rodern. Croom Johnson, c.1938.

Press Directories
Cassey's Directory of Chester, and the Chief Towns in North Wales. Chester: 1876.

Crocker's Wrexham Directory and Postal Guide for 1881–82 … Shrewsbury: W.C. Crocker.

Deacon's Newspaper Handbook and Advertisers' Guide … London: Samuel Deacon & Co, 1881–1895.

Gore's Directory for Liverpool and its environs … Liverpool: J. Mawdsley & Son, 1867.

The Newspaper Press Directory … London: Charles Mitchell, 1851, 1854, 1856–1907.

Selected Bibliography

Porter, Frank. *Postal Directory of Flintshire and Denbighshire, containing classified trade & commercial lists, alphabetically arranged*. Liverpool: Rockliff Brothers, 1886.

The Red Book: and official and trades directory and diary for Wrexham and district, 1892–1893. Wrexham: Woodhall, Minshall, & Thomas.

Sell's Directory of the World's Press, 1883–4. London: Sell's Advertising Offices, 1883.

Slater's Directory of North and Mid Wales. Manchester: Slater's Directories Limited, 1895.

Slater's Royal National Commercial Directory … Manchester: Isaac Slater, 1868.

Slater's Royal National Commercial Directory of North and South Wales … Manchester: Isaac Slater, 1880.

The Wrexham and District Directory, August 1907. Birmingham: Bennett & Co.

Worrall's Directory of North Wales, 1874 … Oldham: John Worrall, 1874.

Wrexham Directory 1886. Hawarden: Clwyd Record Office, 1981 reprint.